WONDER
Doodles

THE *little* BOOK OF
ENCOURAGEMENT, WISDOM & SELF-CARE

JOANNE SHI

 Get Creative 6

ACKNOWLEDGMENTS

To my husband, Eric, my greatest cheerleader and self-proclaimed #1 fan. Thank you for believing in the dream even when I didn't.

To my little boy, Micah. Thank you for reminding me of the beauty of childlike wonder. I hope the message of this book will be one you carry and share with the lost and brokenhearted.

To Jesus. You have been my best friend and greatest teacher of love and kindness. Thank you for it all.

ABOUT THE AUTHOR

JOANNE SHI is a mother, artist, and licensed therapist with a practice in the Bay Area of California. She balances the demands of work and family while dealing with life's ups and downs. Joanne practices being the positive voice you need to keep going when things feel overwhelming through her drawing, writing, and sharing of words of wisdom on her Instagram account @wonder_doodles.

CONTENTS

Introduction 4

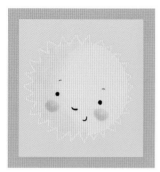

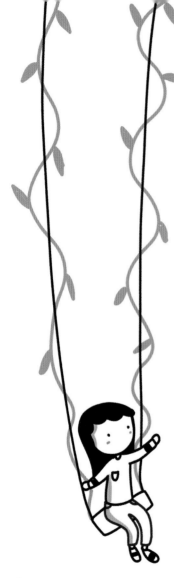

INTRODUCTION

A few years back, a couple of my friends encouraged me to start posting my artwork online. I was going through a difficult season. I was working full time as a mental health therapist and had just moved to the Bay Area for my husband's job. I felt burned out, misplaced, and tired. I remember thinking it was a silly idea, that no one would enjoy it except friends and family, that my work really wasn't good enough. It started as pet portraits and fan art of famous people or accounts I enjoyed and followed on social media, but somewhere in the midst of figuring out my message, mental health came back to the forefront. As I took a step back and looked around me, I realized that there was still so much stigma surrounding mental health, and that a lot of us still couldn't grasp the idea that self-care was not an option—it was a necessity.

I began making artwork that felt close to home with messages of hope and encourage-ment that I personally needed for my life. I needed reminders that it was okay to not be okay, that my well-being mattered, and that I was still worthy even on my hardest and darkest days. I wanted to create artwork that awakened the inner child in all of us, the child that still has so much goodness and hope for the world.

I hope this little book of doodles will do just that. That it will bring light to the darkest places. That it will be a reminder that while life can be incredibly difficult and painful, it can also hold so much good and that this goodness is within each of us. We have the ability to shape our world with kindness and compassion. We have to believe that our existence in this world matters and that we can make a difference.

I'm sure life has thrown its curveballs and twists your way. But you're here! You've survived. Your story is uniquely yours and uniquely beautiful. I hope you are proud of yourself for each new day that you choose to keep going. **I want you to know this simple truth: there will never be another you.** ✳

AFFIRMATIONS

What we choose to think and believe about ourselves is incredibly powerful. A harsh or critical statement that we cling to can wound us for a long time. It can hold us back from the things we want and dream of. It can keep us stuck. On the other hand, an affirmation can produce the opposite effect. It can provoke and encourage us forward and bring sunshine to what might have been a cloudy day. It can be a healing balm to an aching soul.

In my work as a therapist, I often encourage clients to find one affirming statement that they can say about themselves. Often, it's surprisingly hard for them to find one kind thing to say. If I were to ask them for a list of things they felt they needed to work on, many of them might come up with a laundry list of what they believe are their shortcomings.

Affirmations are not an attempt to ignore or hide the things we want to improve. They are not a way to pretend that everything about us is perfect, nor a way to puff ourselves up. Affirmations are a way of speaking tenderly and nudging ourselves or others forward. Imagine what the often harsh or critical thoughts you speak to yourself would do to someone else if you were to direct them toward them. Speak to yourself the way you would to a friend you deeply care about. If they deserve your tenderness, then so do you.

These are also not one-off statements but words we need to repeat to ourselves over and over again— particularly on the extra-rough days. We have the power to choose to speak life over ourselves, rather than death. If you find yourself having a hard time, just look at yourself in the mirror and say, **"You're doing okay!"** Others won't always say the words to us but we can be our own greatest cheer-leaders and advocates. *

YOUR TOUGHEST DAYS DO NOT DEFINE YOUR VALUE.

THE NEXT TIME YOU FEEL STUCK... LOOK BACK + SEE HOW FAR YOU'VE TRULY COME.

DEAR ME,
   YOU HAVE SURVIVED
THE HARDEST DAYS,
ENDURED GREAT
   PAINS + HEARTACHES,
WALKED THROUGH
   DISAPPOINTMENT,
LIVED THROUGH
   GRIEF.

YOU ARE DOING YOUR BEST
   AND THAT'S ENOUGH.

♡, ME

life is TOUGH
BUT SO ARE YOU.

YOU'VE SURVIVED
100%
OF YOUR WORST DAYS.

BAD DAYS
SURVIVAL EXAM   (100)

1. _____
   _____

2. _____
   _____

KEEP GOING

IT'S OKAY IF SOME DAYS YOU'RE JUST HANGING ON AS BEST AS YOU CAN.

21

You are worthy of the most BEAUTIFUL things.

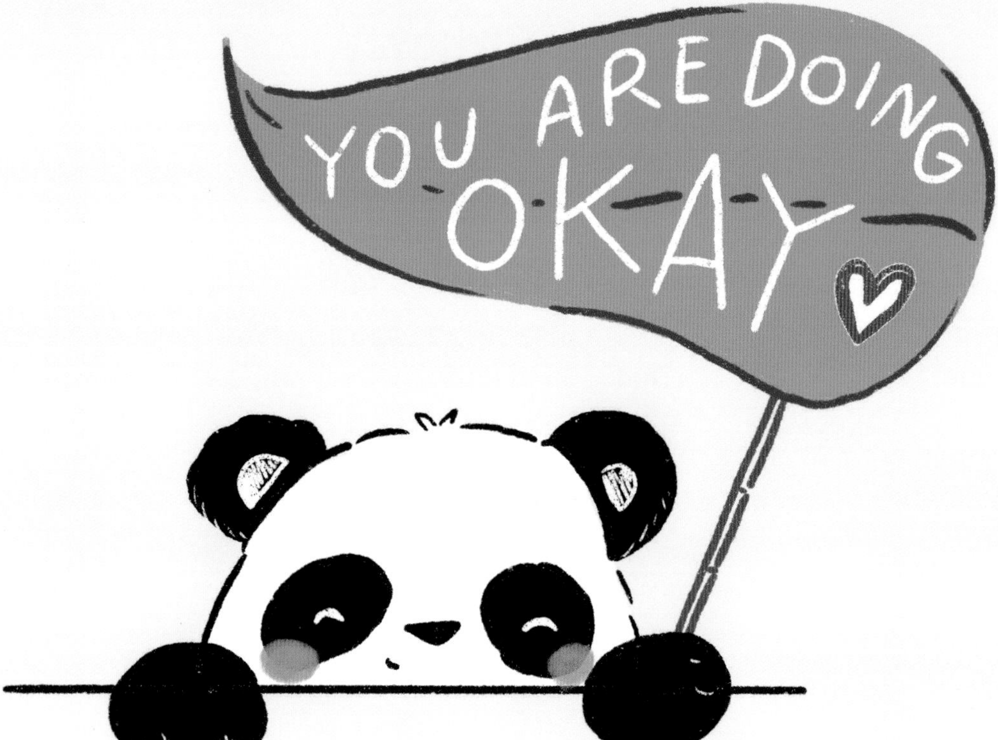
YOU ARE DOING
OKAY

I TRIED MY BEST TODAY

AND THAT'S GOOD ENOUGH

Kindness is truly one of the most important aspects of our humanity. One of my favorite quotes is, "Be kind. For everyone you meet is going through their own battle." If we think about it, all of us are just trying our best to make it through the highs and the lows of life. We're all people with strengths and weaknesses. We all have personal pains and struggles, and I'm a firm believer that if we all practice greater kindness, the world would be a better place.

Race, religion, political affiliation, outer appearance, age. . . No matter how different it may be from our own, we have to be willing to cross those lines and extend kindness to all, ourselves included.

Have you ever encountered someone with road rage, or maybe you've been guilty of a little rage of your own? Or maybe a loved one was unkind? Maybe someone you knew made a mean remark about you. I'm sure you can remember how horrible those moments felt. You can probably remember the ways that little moments like those have ruined your day.

Now, have you ever encountered a time when someone was simply kind to you? Maybe a friend or loved one spoke an encouraging word. Perhaps someone at the grocery store helped you with your bags, or someone in the line at the coffee shop paid for your coffee. Or maybe it was as simple as someone giving you a smile and a friendly hello. I'm sure you remember how sweet those moments felt. Moments like that can change our day from dark and dreary to hopeful and light. They make us see the good around us. And mend the parts of us that are hurting.

That's the power of kindness, and here's the best part: it's free and yours to give over and over again. So, when things feel chaotic or hopeless, I challenge you to go spread a little kindness and to notice the kindness around you. **I promise that something inside you will shift.** *

JUST A LITTLE
BIT OF KINDNESS
TOWARD YOURSELF
CAN GO A LONG WAY

WE need EACH OTHER

SOMETIMES A
SILENT HUG
IS THE ONLY
THING TO SAY.

PLANTING
EVEN JUST
ONE SEED
OF Kindness
CAN MAKE A
DIFFERENCE.

IN TIMES
OF
CHAOS,

SPREADING
Kindness
STILL MAKES
A DIFFERENCE.

OF ALL THE THINGS WE
COULD BE KNOWN FOR...
LET KINDNESS BE
THE MARK WE LEAVE
BE HIND.

WAYS TO SHOW
Kindness

WRITE
AN
ENCOURAGING
NOTE

CALL & CHECK IN
ON SOMEONE JUST
BECAUSE

OFFER TO HELP
SOMEONE

TREAT SOMEONE
TO COFFEE

YOU'RE
AWESOME!

COMPLIMENT
SOMEONE

SMILE!

love well
EVEN WHEN
YOU'RE NOT
well loved.

In a world
where you
can be
any-thing,

BE

KIND.

KINDNESS BRINGS
light TO THE
DARKEST PLACES.

HOW MAGICAL THAT KINDNESS IS FREE. GIVE IT WITH NO FEAR.

LET THEM KNOW YOU'RE THINKING OF THEM

ENCOURAGE THEM TO SEEK HELP

LISTEN

HOW TO HELP SOMEONE WHO IS STRUGGLING

MAKE A PLAN WITH THEIR LOVED ONES

VALIDATE THEIR FEELINGS

OFFER TO HELP WITH SOME SIMPLE TASKS

BE PRESENT + PATIENT

ASK HOW YOU CAN HELP

'BE KIND EVEN ON YOUR WORST DAYS.

AN ACT
OF
KINDNESS
CAN TURN
A TOUGH
DAY INTO A
GOOD ONE.

A
HOPEFUL
reminder

I recently started focusing my doodles on the idea of hope, because I was finding that hope often feels scarce in present-day society.

I wanted people to know that hope is never lost and that it truly is our life source. It's what keeps us going in the midst of the hardships and pain we all face. That's the thing I've learned about life. Life never promised to be free of difficulties. It never promised we will not experience pain. We have to believe that even though it's hard, there are beautiful moments. We have to believe that wonderful and good things are still possible and that there is a purpose in everything we experience.

I think a lot of us need more hope in our lives. With everything happening in the world, we all need extra bits of light in the darkness. Do you know that hope is associated with greater happiness, academic achievement, and a lowered risk of death? Hope is not some magical feeling that will cure all our pain, but I think that hope can change the lens through which we see life. It's a lens that allows us to focus on the good. To not carry the bad with us. It's a lens that helps us see the rainbows that will surely come after the rain.

I don't know what your life looks like right now. Maybe things are generally going well, and that's wonderful. But maybe you're in a place where you need a reminder of hope. Maybe you've had a series of bad days, weeks, or years and you feel like you're losing against life. Maybe the pain has been with you for so long that there's not much left within you to keep going. I'm here to tell you this:

You matter.
Good things can still happen.
Don't give up. *

EVEN IN YOUR DARKEST NIGHT

THE STARS ARE STILL SHINING

SOMETIMES THE HARDEST RAINS BRING THE MOST BEAUTIFUL RAINBOWS

Beautiful
THINGS
CAN
GROW OUT
OF
hardship

REFUSE TO SURRENDER YOUR HOPE

52

SOMEONE YOU ARE THANKFUL FOR
ONE GOOD THING THAT HAPPENED RECENTLY
HOPEFUL THOUGHTS
ALL THE WAYS THINGS CAN GO RIGHT
PAST VICTORIES
A GOOD DEED

HOLD ON TO THE GOOD STUFF.

NO MATTER HOW CLOUDY THE DAYS GET, I WILL NEVER STOP LOOKING FOR THE sun.

NEVER STOP HOPING FOR GOOD THINGS

HOPE

NOUN

1. A FEELING OF EXPECTATION AND DESIRE FOR A CERTAIN THING TO HAPPEN

2. A FEELING OF TRUST

EACH DAY BRINGS NEW HOPE

IT WON'T ALWAYS FEEL THIS WAY.

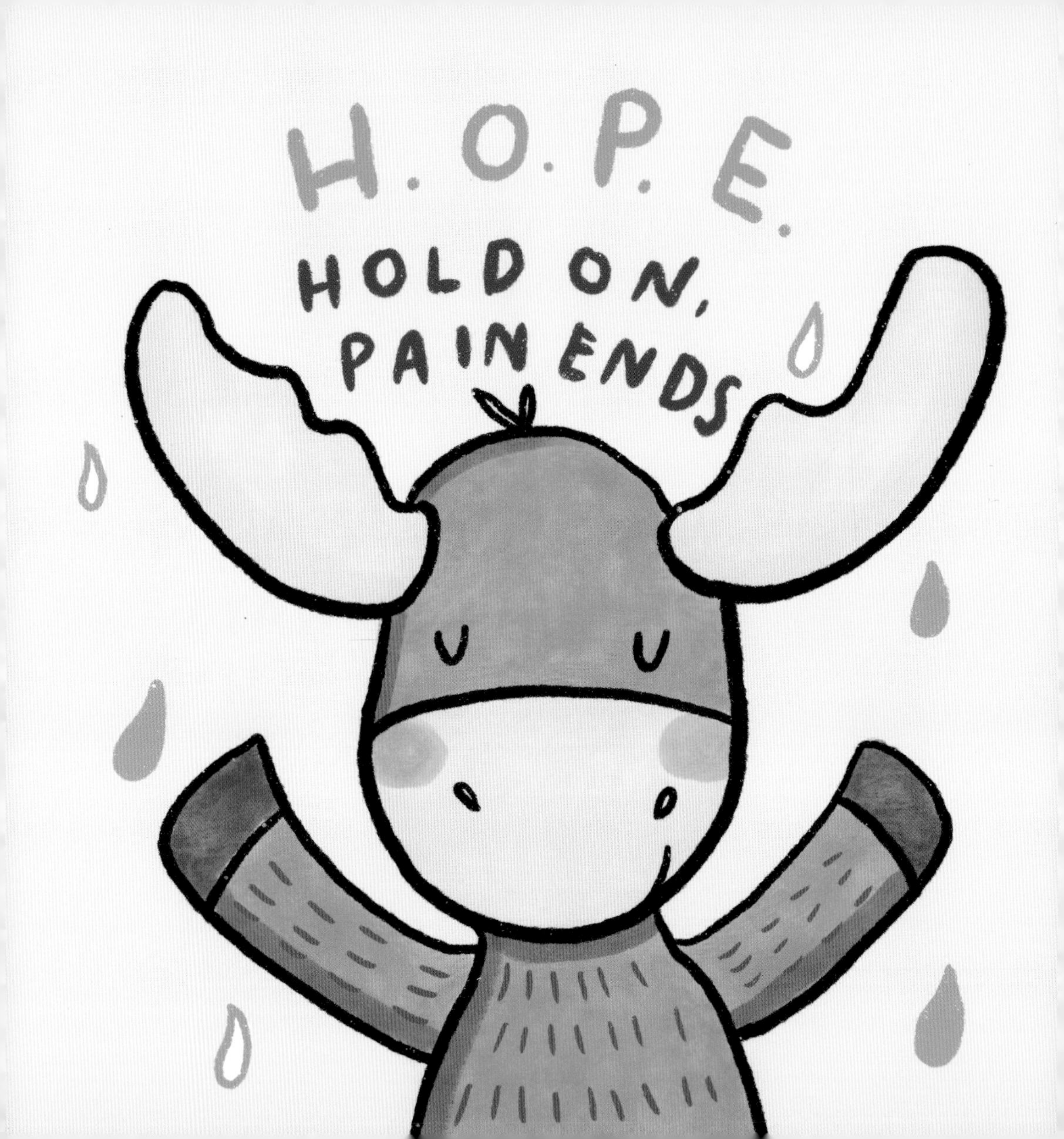
H.O.P.E.
HOLD ON, PAIN ENDS

THE BLOOMS OF THE FUTURE REST IN THE SEEDS YOU CHOOSE TO PLANT TODAY.

you can't
always see
growth
BUT IT DOESN'T
MEAN IT'S NOT
HAPPENING.

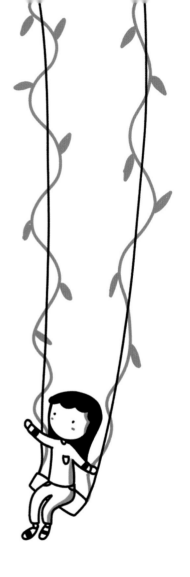

WAYS TO INCREASE HOPE

- ACKNOWLEDGE YOUR STRENGTHS

- PRAY OR MEDITATE

- PRACTICE CONSISTENT SELF-CARE

- JOURNAL

- VOLUNTEER OR DO SOMETHING FOR SOMEONE ELSE

- REMEMBER YOUR RESOURCES

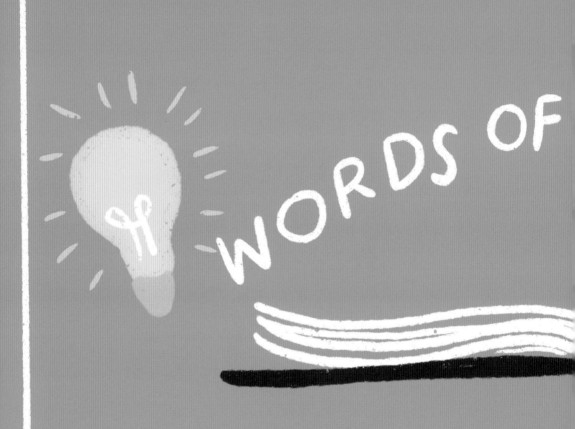

The first step to growth is to acknowledge that you don't have all the answers. This is why I find that seeking the wisdom of those who have gone before us is incredibly powerful and encouraging. There are so many heroes and role models who inspire. Ones who have championed and led movements leading to greater equality and freedom for mankind. Ones who quietly and lovingly cared for the poor and needy. Those who innovated and created things we had never dreamed of. Ones who were forerunners in their fields. Dreamers. Go-getters. World-changers.

There are also those who work continually to be powerful voices in the present and to pave the way for a brighter future. Whether it's with their work, charisma, humor, or ability to connect and understand human pain and triumph, these voices carry wisdom that we can all use on a daily basis. On the days when I feel discouraged, I often think about these heroes and imagine how challenging some of their circumstances have been and how they persevered anyway and held on to what they believed in and worked for. It stirs my courage and resolve to keep moving forward and believing that the things I hope for can be achieved.

When you're having a tough day or you just don't know where to go next, I think it's helpful to find these voices and stand on the foundation they've built for us. They were and are still human, after all, with their own struggles and victories, highs and lows. It's always humbling to see that there is still so much we can do for those around us and our world—but also encouraging to know that our personal struggles are not enough to keep us down if we don't let them. I think **we can find hope and enlightenment in their words,** and they can light our path when the way seems dim. ✳

CHOOSE ONE BRAVE THING TO DO TODAY

COURAGE JAR

KIND WORDS
CAN BE SHORT &
EASY TO SPEAK,
BUT THEIR ECHOES
ARE TRULY
ENDLESS —MOTHER TERESA

DARKNESS CANNOT
DRIVE OUT DARKNESS;
ONLY *light* CAN DO
THAT.
HATE CANNOT DRIVE
OUT HATE;
ONLY *love* CAN DO
THAT.
— MLK JR

REFLECTION

THINK OF ONE OF
YOUR GREATEST HEROES
AND INFLUENCES...

HOW CAN THEY
INSPIRE OR ENCOURAGE
YOU TODAY?

FOR BEAUTIFUL EYES,
LOOK FOR THE GOOD IN OTHERS;
FOR BEAUTIFUL LIPS,
SPEAK ONLY
WORDS OF
KINDNESS;
AND FOR POISE,
WALK WITH THE
KNOWLEDGE
THAT YOU ARE
NEVER ALONE
- AUDREY
HEPBURN

I KEEP MY IDEALS,
BECAUSE IN SPITE OF EVERYTHING
I STILL BELIEVE THAT PEOPLE
ARE REALLY GOOD AT HEART.
        -ANNE FRANK

I NEVER
LOSE.
I EITHER
WIN
OR
LEARN.
— NELSON MANDELA

THERE ARE THREE WAYS
TO ULTIMATE SUCCESS.
THE FIRST WAY IS TO
BE KIND.
THE SECOND WAY IS TO
BE KIND.
THE THIRD WAY IS TO
BE KIND.
- FRED ROGERS

turn YOUR
wounds
INTO wisdom
-OPRAH
WINFREY

FIND OUT WHO YOU
ARE AND DO IT
ON PURPOSE
- DOLLY PARTON

EVERY
ACCOMPLISHMENT
STARTS WITH
THE DECISION
TO TRY.
—JFK

Courage
CHALLENGE

CHOOSE ONE BRAVE THING TO DO TODAY

COURAGE JAR

EVERY GREAT DREAM BEGINS WITH A DREAMER. ALWAYS REMEMBER, YOU HAVE WITHIN YOU THE STRENGTH, THE PATIENCE + THE PASSION TO REACH FOR THE STARS TO CHANGE THE WORLD.
~ HARRIET TUBMAN

YOU MUST
BE THE
CHANGE
YOU WISH TO
SEE IN THE
WORLD
-GANDHI

THE BEST + MOST BEAUTIFUL THINGS IN THE WORLD CANNOT BE SEEN OR EVEN TOUCHED. THEY MUST BE FELT WITH THE *heart*.

- HELEN KELLER

YOU MUST
NEVER BE FEARFUL
ABOUT WHAT YOU
ARE DOING WHEN
IT IS RIGHT.
–ROSA PARKS

SUCCESS IS NOT FINAL; FAILURE IS NOT FATAL. IT IS THE courage TO CONTINUE THAT COUNTS. — WINSTON CHURCHILL

YOU MAY NOT CONTROL
ALL THE EVENTS
THAT HAPPEN TO YOU,
BUT YOU CAN
DECIDE NOT TO BE
REDUCED BY THEM.
– MAYA ANGELOU

Ah, self-care. A term that has become more and more popular. As a therapist, it's one of the first things I recommend to my clients and an ongoing theme throughout our therapy journey. Why? Because I've found that many of us put self-care at the bottom of our priority list, when in reality it should be at the top. We are prone to forgetting that we are not superhuman and that we all need rest and tenderness from time to time. People come back and tell me, "I tried it and it didn't work." I usually ask follow-up questions that reveal that they usually didn't try it for a consistent period of time, or they didn't put much effort or thought into what they actually wanted to do as self-care.

Self-care doesn't have to be complicated, time consuming, or expensive. It's just about carving out some intentional time and space to care for yourself. Finding time to check in with yourself and see how you're truly feeling—and replenishing the areas that need a refill. So many of us wait until our tanks are on empty and we're running on fumes, which only leads to burnout and less joy.

Why do we put ourselves last? We often think that self-care is not really beneficial. I was someone who felt like it was too indulgent, and I couldn't see that self-care is a discipline and something that I have to practice to see its long-term benefits.

We've been trained to think that caring for ourselves is self-centered. But I encourage you to remember that self-care is for yourself *and* for everyone around you. I know when I'm burned out, I'm less efficient, less loving, less present, and quicker to anger, tire, and become discouraged . . .

Need I continue? When I'm filled up, I'm more the person I want to be than when I've run myself dry.

So, repeat after me:

"I will not feel guilty for taking care of myself."

"I will not put myself last."

"I am allowed to rest."

Now, go do it! ✳

POURING INTO YOURSELF
IS SOMETHING YOU
NEVER NEED TO APOLOGIZE
FOR.

BELLY-BREATHING
EXERCISE

1. SIT OR LIE IN A COMFY SPOT.
2. PUT ONE HAND ON YOUR BELLY & THE OTHER ON YOUR CHEST.
3. TAKE A BREATH THROUGH YOUR NOSE & PUSH BELLY OUT.
4. BREATHE OUT THROUGH MOUTH LIKE YOU'RE WHISTLING. (REPEAT!)

nourish to
flourish

I AM CONVINCED THAT THERE IS NO BETTER DAY THAN *today* TO START "*yes*" SAYING TO ME.

THERE IS ALWAYS TIME FOR A DEEP BREATH

ASKING FOR HELP IS NOT WEAKNESS

YOU DON'T NEED TO JUSTIFY TAKING CARE OF YOURSELF

TAKE THE TIME YOU NEED

Don't FEEL GUILTY FOR TAKING CARE OF you

CRYING CAN BE self-care TOO

SELF-CARE REMINDERS

MAKE self-care A HABIT

YOU'LL BE MORE PRODUCTIVE WHEN YOU'RE filled up

BE KIND TO YOURSELF ON THE HARD DAYS.

THE ART OF CHECKING IN

- [ ] TAKE A DEEP BREATH

- [ ] HOW AM I FEELING?

- [ ] ARE THERE ANY ACHES OR PAINS IN MY BODY?

- [ ] IS THERE ANYTHING THAT HAPPENED TODAY THAT NEEDS SOME EXTRA THOUGHT & REFLECTION?

SOMETIMES A NICE WALK OUTSIDE IS JUST WHAT YOU NEED

If you make a list of things that are within your control and a list of things that are not, you'll find one list will be significantly shorter than the other. There are many things in our lives that we have no control over, but we think that if we hold on tighter we'll somehow gain control.

Maybe you're finding that your brain is constantly running and riddled with worry. Maybe you're noticing aches and pains in your body from all of the tension and stress you're carrying. It may be time to let go. To remind yourself that letting go can be incredibly freeing.

Letting go is one of my bigger struggles. For a long time, letting go felt like I was admitting defeat in difficult situations. I've learned that letting go doesn't mean defeat. It means that I'm accepting that situations come as they will and I have the confidence that no matter what they look like, I can make it through.

Whether you need to relinquish control over a certain situation or you need to let go of the past or a criticism, you'll find that if you open your hands, they will be ready to hold on to the better things.

For a greater part of my life, I've held on to a lot of ideas that didn't serve me well. To name just a few:

- Emotions and crying are signs of weakness.
- I'm a failure if I mess up, even just once.
- My feelings aren't valid or important.
- I have to always stay in control of everything around me.
- It's my job to fix everything and everyone.

. . . and the list goes on and on. I don't think I'm alone in these thoughts either.

Over time, I've learned it's a journey to keep letting go of these misconceptions. It's a daily commitment to try to live as freely and genuinely as I can. So, if you're ready to let go, commit to it wholeheartedly and **see what new places it can take you.** ✳

SOMETIMES FREEDOM IS ON THE OTHER SIDE OF LETTING GO

IT'S OKAY TO FALL APART.

tacos fall apart
AND WE STILL LOVE
THEM.

SOMETIMES WE NEED TO BE STILL
TO KEEP MOVING FORWARD

NONE OF US HAS EVERYTHING
FIGURED OUT AND
THAT'S ABSOLUTELY
OKAY.

THERE WILL ALWAYS
BE MESSY THINGS IN
OUR WORLD AND OUR LIVES.
AFTER ALL, WHEN DID GROWTH,
CHANGE, AND PROGRESS
EVER COME FROM PERFECTION?

SOME DAYS ALL
YOU CAN DO
IS JUST KEEP
BREATHING.

SOMETIMES WE HAVE TO LET GO OF THE OLD THINGS TO MAKE ROOM FOR THE NEW.

WHEN YOU FEEL OVERWHELMED

1) TAKE A DEEP BREATH

2) NAME 5 THINGS YOU CAN *SEE*

3) NAME 4 THINGS YOU CAN *TOUCH*

4) NAME 3 THINGS YOU CAN *HEAR*

5) NAME 2 THINGS YOU CAN *SMELL*

6) FIND ONE THING TO TASTE

THIS IS CALLED GROUNDING. ENGAGING YOUR SENSES CAN HELP YOU CENTER YOURSELF IN THE PRESENT, SLOW DOWN YOUR MIND + HELP INCREASE SELF-AWARENESS.

It's okay to enjoy LIFE even when THINGS AREN'T PERFECT.

WHAT I CAN'T CONTROL

WHAT I CAN CONTROL

PICK A SITUATION
YOU ARE IN
THAT FEELS TOUGH
AND REMIND
YOURSELF OF THE
THINGS YOU
CAN & CAN'T
CONTROL

CIRCLE OF CONTROL

I DON'T HAVE TO CONTROL EVERYTHING TO BE OKAY.

I CAN'T CONTROL EVERYTHING
THAT HAPPENS,
BUT I ALWAYS GET TO CHOOSE
MY NEXT STEPS.

Get Creative 6

An imprint of
Mixed Media Resources
19 West 21st Street, Suite 601
New York, NY 10010
sixthandspringbooks.com

Senior Editor
MICHELLE BREDESON

Acquisitions Editor
B.J. BERTI

Design Director
IRENE LEDWITH

Book Design
DIANE LAMPHRON

Chief Executive Officer
CAROLINE KILMER

President
ART JOINNIDES

Chairman
JAY STEIN

Library of Congress Cataloging-in-Publication Data is available upon request.

ISBN: 978-1-68462-043-2

Manufactured in China

1 3 5 7 9 10 8 6 4 2

First Edition